An expedition of the soul: My journey to self discovery!

Sweedel Nisha Dsa

BookLeaf Publishing

India | USA | UK

Presentation by *BookLeaf Publishing*

Web: www.bookleafpub.com

E-mail: info@bookleafpub.com

ISBN:9789358318708

First edition 2024

DEDICATION

To all the youngsters and families who have suffered and are suffering from violence, I hope you receive the freedom and justice you deserve. God bless you all.

ACKNOWLEDGEMENT

Firstly, I thank God Almighty for giving me the gift of life, and the situations that I faced, due to which this book is possible today.

Secondly, I am extremely grateful to my amazing middle sister, Sharal Niveditha Dsa, who is one of my biggest role models for her support and encouragement towards this book. This book was fully possible due to her enthusiasm and dedication as she had introduced me to this great publishing platform that I have published this book through. Also, I thank BookLeaf Publishing for giving new writers like me an opportunity to shine and share their efforts to the world.

Lastly, I thank my lovely mother, father and my eldest sister for their love, understanding, generosity and care towards the formation of my first poetry book. I also thank all my well-wishers who guided me throughout my journey of self-discovery.

Thank you, my dear readers, for your time and curiosity. God bless you all.

PREFACE

This book is a collection of my experiences of life; both the beauty and the trauma in it, and how I discovered myself through this journey called life.

Since childhood, my mother and middle sister loved writing their feelings down in the form of poems; maybe creative writing just flowed in our blood. Although they did it rarely as I grew up, poetry stuck with me and I was good with what I wrote.

Age is just a number, and experiences are not defined by age. Thus, I would like to share my poems regarding life, especially my life; how I was abused, and how I believed in myself to change the situation.

I hope this book inspires you to look through your life and be grateful for the trials you face, to let yourself know that nothing is impossible, and to love and discover yourself.

The World Of My Mind

The world of my mind,
It shall be loving and kind.
It is for the one who deserves it,
the purpose of humanity; he serves it.

To find eternal peace,
from this world which shall cease.
To finally feel free,
like the swinging roots of the banyan tree.

Where there is no judgement or mourning,
because the state of today's world feels
concerning.
Where we find happy people, smiling faces,
no competitions, marathons or races.

Only love from the heavens above,
and no argument about what and how?
I wish there is such a world,
where there will be justice even to a bird.

This is the beautiful world of my mind,
which I am sure will take a million years to find.

A Perfect Family

I always wanted to have a perfect family;
A perfect father, a perfect mother,
and perfect sisters, with a perfect me.

I thought it was having all sorts of joy,
goodness, health and wealth,
all the time in our family, every day.

What I realised as days passed,
that this could never be true;
No matter how hard I tried.

That no family was perfect.
That we all have our own lives and stories,
that we are all imperfect.

We can give it our best shot;
but assuring if it will work or not,
would be left up to fate.

I now think that being imperfect is the real joy,
the real goodness, the real trials,
that take place in our family every day.

An Apple and A Tomato

My sisters, I love them so much!
I was tiny, like a speck in their hands.
Those two 11- and 13-year-olds seemed
confident in describing the newborn in their
arms.

'Wow, she looks like an apple!'
'No. She resembles a tomato!'
All this was due to my rosy little cheeks;
And these were the first thoughts
of my two amazing pseudo moms.

We grew up together; of course
fate made them older than me.
Maybe it was decided, that
a baby would have two guardian angels,
And when she was wise enough,
she would be their guardian angel.

This miniscule creature went
wherever it was taken, carried on their waist.
The joy when people adored me;
They thought of me as their young one.

They played with me, gave me piggybacks,

bathed me, fed me, this list had no end.
I loved sleeping in the centre;
where my one leg was on one of them,
and the other was pushed outside the sleeping
mat.

Where poor miss got bitten,
by mosquitoes outside the sleeping net.
They loved me, even with all the mischiefs
I was not aware of, being a deep sleeper.
And our holidays were complete, only when
they
were forced to play quizzes, my favourite.

I still remember the days
when one of them lifted me,
flipping me upside down.
I wish they still could, it was so fun.

Through all this, it was so hard
to see them cry, with all the sufferings.
They were, and still are, my true best friends.
and I can say to this day, that I still
haven't found anyone like them.

To differentiate, although difficult,
My eldest sister is 'Mi madre'
And my middle sister, 'Ma mère'.
both, part of my soul, inseparable.

They really never let me feel alone,
but waving adieu was so heartbreaking.

Time passed, they had to leave home.
The little bundle of joy they once saw,
has now grown older; but it misses them
dearly, it feels like I have lost myself.

Those days are deeply yearned, even now.
They protected her, she was safe and loved,
just like when she went crying about something;
or when she came joyfully laughing,
and they celebrated and encouraged her.

I would not mind going back to day 'one',
as these pure souls were deciding if
I was an apple or a tomato.
I would not mind giving up my everything for
them.
I know that they would still make me shine,
to make me succeed nonetheless.

Because to them, I was their brightest star,
the sweetest apple, and the most flavourful
tomato.

A Mother's Tremor

The night is calm,
the wind is shushed.
It is cold outside with a weary of darkness,
in sleeps my baby, lovingly hushed.

But something in my heart,
awaits me haughtily.
My conscience is disturbed wildly,
the weather calls out to me, dauntingly.

Thunder roars,
lightning strikes.
The wind runs in despair;
my baby cries.

The darkness shines,
the clouds brightly chime.
I am worried dearly,
nature has committed its crime.

My house, it is not so strong,
my family is in danger.
They are unable to sleep properly,
my baby, is it safe in the manger?

The Anguish Of A Broken Soul

The reign of terror, the rise of fear,
the tears before I fell asleep, with every uttered prayer.
How scared I was, how broken I felt,
how terrified I was, in anxiety I knelt.

Every word I spoke, I interrogated myself prior.
I was worried, was it okay to state a desire?
Afraid of getting beaten up, abused,
both physically and mentally, scratched and bruised.

The distress and anguish, oh my unbearable torment,
the unending depression, the furious embarrassment,
which added to the victimization, felt like endless 'why's, a mystery
full of confusions, suffering and utmost misery.

With every action, criticised, I estimated my worth,
I questioned God. What was the purpose of my birth?

All I heard back then was curses and arguments,
in the process of which, were disregarded my
sentiments.

The despair in my situation, now as I write in
brief,
I truly say, words cannot suffice to describe this
grief!
My household items turned into weapons for
violence,
and painful deafening screams were
overpowered by a terrifying silence.

My childhood, it saw injured humans with
scarred souls,
With marks that hurt more than their hearts
which had holes;
that they carved to let their pain outflow,
or else, if expressed, might lead to a death blow.

The horror in my eyes, my cheeks were flooded,
the dread as they saw the hands that were
blooded.
The place I slept in, was the same place where I
was awake and wounded,
with no one to save me, I wish my life had
ended,
but maybe, just maybe, a greater purpose, for me
it was intended.

Loving Her

She absolutely hated herself.
To her, she was the most imperfect,
lazy and useless being who deserved nothing.
But to me, she was beautiful,
and all she needed was a little bit of love.

I convinced her she was amazing.
She was the most caring,
the kindest person I had ever seen,
but she wanted to be perfect.
She wanted to be able to do everything.

She was real, so she thought the same for all.
Was not everyone real and truthful too?
Their lies, jealousy and bullying broke her.
She taught others to appreciate their scars,
but hers did not seem like scars to herself.

She was the brightest and smartest.
She smiled like a newborn baby
to everyone around her who hated her joy.
They wanted to make her feel empty,
but she did not know she could feel it too.

Her circumstances made her cry.

She liked the fact that her cheeks glowed
when she cried those tears out
as she saw herself in the mirror,
maybe as she tried to change that pain to love.

She was told she was 'chubbier' than others.
They told her to eat well, and she did.
So, they commented on her; on that child
who smiled at them knowing all sort of pain.
She definitely knew it more than love.

I told her, 'Gosh, you are beautiful.'
She replied, 'Oh no, I am disgusting.'
I told her, 'Your intelligence is admired by
many!'
She replied, 'Oh, it is nothing.'
That is how she brushed off my compliments.

She did not know she deserved it all.
Unknown to the fact that her uniqueness
was of the finest pearl - so natural, so rare.
I gave her some years to ponder on this.
So, she took that time, using it for the better.

People taught her she was trash and used her.
Yet, she loved, loved with no limits;
she was exhausted and overwhelmed.
When she turned to me for advice,
I suggested her to give that same love to herself.

Over time, she started accepting my
compliments.
 Again, I told her, 'Gosh, you are so pretty.'
She replied, 'Wow, really pretty.'
I told her, 'Your confidence is admired by
many.'
She replied, 'Isn't it so wonderful?'

That response was so amazing to me.
Even though sometimes it is difficult,
Yet she is doing great now.
I love her, she is my darling.
She says, this world is beautiful with her in it.

I took time, but I healed her.
It was hard to accept, or maybe agree
when I told her that I loved her;
When she told me that I was her,
and that she was me.

The Face Or The Hand?

The face bubbling with anger;
It was a sign of destruction.
The wait for the storm to subside,
oh, the terrorizing expression.

The face that was joyful,
it was the one that worried about my safety.
The teacher of hardwork and knowledge,
oh, how it seemed so great to me.

The hand that hit me hard,
it was truly heart breaking cruelty.
The grabbing of my face that was supposed to
shush me,
oh, how those nails scratched me unknowingly.

The hand that nurtured with love,
it fed me till my stomach was full.
The spot of kajal put on my cheeks,
oh, I was cared for to perfection.

The face that smiled at me,
was the same face that yelled till I cried.
The face that would die for me,
was the same face that was ready to kill.

The hand that brought me up,
was the same hand that pulled me down.
The hand that blessed me,
was the same hand being raised to curse.

Was I suppose to love that face,
or utterly despise that hand;
or was I supposed to hold that hand,
and deeply hate that face?
they fed me and tore me altogether,
was it something I was supposed to withstand?

Inquisition!

What a range of notions?
What a story portraying emotion?
What is this, what is that?
What a place full of commotion?

Who was crying, who laughed?
Who was leaving, and who came?
Who is this, who is that?
Who was this person, can I know their name?

When did she hear this song?
When did this world begin to cease?
When is this, when is that?
When did my heart find peace?

Where are my socks, my shoes?
Where are the bowls for ice cream?
Where is this, where is that?
Where are the parents of the baby that screams?

How to play the keyboard chords?
How to stop wanting to be perfect?
How is this, how is that?
How to make a difference, a positive effect?

So many questions, some stay unanswered,
but not all of them would really need answers.
Many of them, though answered,
start a new set of questions;
Which may one day end with a reply,
without searching for another answer, or asking
some more questions.

Another Tiring Day

Day and night,
this feeling will remain.
Having a sleepy sight,
My weak body is in pain.

People think it is laziness,
when actually it is not.
Oh, my dear God, bless
me working while it is so hot.

My brain is wired,
with a mind so exhausted.
My body is tired,
all over I feel so rusted.

This makes my thoughts,
so very negative.
My liveliness rots;
Nothing stays positive.

I feel so astray.
Not knowing what to say,
slowly I sleep; down I lay,
waking up to another tiring day.

My Dear Youth

My dear youth,
let me spread my wings!
May it touch the heart
of the bird that sings.

My dear youth,
let me perceive being free!
May it release the suffering
of every chained soul wanting to flee.

My dear youth,
let me persist as just!
May it make in this world
truth and kindness a must.

My dear youth,
let me triumph as positive!
May it spark in every being
the endurance and need to live.

My dear youth,
let me hold on to my confidence!
May it give rise in the people
the courage to display their essence.

My dear youth,
let me fulfil my responsibility!
May it withstand hurdles, and
give me the chance to showcase my ability.

My dear youth,
let me build my character!
May it make my nation feel
that I am its protector.

My dear youth,
let me shine being kind!
May it ablaze a difference
to each sorrowful, downcast mind.

My dear youth,
let me bring warmth in the cold!
May it offer a loving shoulder
that commemorates the strength of the bold.

My dear youth,
let me manifest care!
May it be a new beginning,
a pledge to selflessly share.

The Description Of Love

Love is so pure,
it is so fine.
It surely has happiness;
like the sweetness of age-old wine.

The candle melting itself,
is a form of love, a sacrifice.
It has given itself;
so that real love can suffice.

The birds chirping up above,
sing to make everyone joyful.
The sweetness it has is love,
meaningful and merciful.

The rainbow in the sky,
shows a sign of love.
With flying colours so high,
and a snow-white dove.

These tiny things show me
the goodness all around.
All over is love I see;
leaving me so astound.

Goodbye, My Dear

When I am away from you,
I miss your presence deeply;
and now as you say goodbye,
I cannot stop, but cry.

There were times of joy,
when we cared and shared.
As we go apart, my dear one,
I hope you will not forget our memories, none.

I still love you always,
you can sincerely open up to me.
Although I do not know your reason to part,
yet undoubtedly, you are in my heart.

Never will be the day,
I stop thinking about our times of life.
I yearn to stay with you, forever.
Wishing you a good life,
I wish I did not have to say, that unfortunate
goodbye.

The Perfect Woman In Society

Always smiling shows her beauty,
bad styling makes her dirty,
housework is her duty.
Is this the woman you want, society?

Short clothes make her a slut,
covered body, yet you call her hot,
her emotions are a worthless dot.
Is this the woman you want, society?

Abusing her is just so easy,
judging her has made you busy,
blaming her saying she is fussy.
Is this the woman you want, society?

Forbidden to every choice,
soft-spoken must be her voice,
with a never revealing body poise.
Is this the woman you want, society?

Tied up must be her hair,
her life must never be fair,
she gets nothing from her share.
Is this the woman you want, society?

No looking at men,
her discipline must be ten on ten,
her periods are a sin.
Is this the woman you want, society?

Her home is her cage,
her life is that of a sage,
she can never be enraged.
Is this the woman you want, society?

Marrying her off is most important,
she is like a burden, a heavy rent,
anger is on her always vent.
Is this the woman you want, society?

Kids are her responsibility,
cooking must be her best ability,
she is considered like a utility.
Is this the woman you want, society?

Her opinions never matter,
her heart is meant to shatter,
her laughter or tears both must stutter.
Is this the woman you want, society?

Her fault is being born,
her soul, scratched off and worn,
her dreams must be torn.
Is this the woman you want, society?

The Power Of Words

It was a secret.
A secret that would shake the person
Who was not supposed to know it.

It was done with absolute care;
No trace done found as it was carried out.
It was serious, it felt like sin.

To see a change, to make a difference,
Or more so to survive,
As it was accomplished with tears of sacrifice.

An act to frighten the oppressor,
by the one who was oppressed;
It was done with courage that overpowered fear.

It was scary, very scary.
Silent conversations, panicked movements,
with unpredictable results, for an unpredictable
future.

It was a legal action, a complaint
to the police, about domestic violence.
I still remember the bloody clothes which I took
as proof.

My mother took the responsibility,
to make sure I was not harmed.
But as time passed, it would be revealed.

I forced my family members,
I wanted to be free.
I could not bear the violence anymore.

I was going crazier,
Unable to bear the fact
that we were victimized just for being alive.

The one who did not know to lie,
had to pretend, so that she would not die.
I was experiencing the worst anxiety.

It was a lot to process.
The action scared the oppressor,
but did not change his identity.

I fought with him,
With tears in eyes, with regret in my heart.
With emptiness in my soul, I did not know to
hurt.

The child that was supposed
to be taught to live with humans,
taught humanity to the one who gave her life.

I was shattered explaining someone how to be
human,
when I did not feel like one myself.
It had to be done for the lives of my people.

Every time I stood in between
when that beating was about to strike my
mother,
so that it would at least be disrupted.

It got better as time marched on.
We did not give up,
And eventually, we started winning the battle.

Prayers were not enough; tears were not enough.
Only words were, because all he needed to
change,
was knowing how humans really feel.

He was the best friend of the world,
but an enemy of his family.
I knew I would not win immediately, but
definitely.

Maybe it was just his upbringing
or that he did not get enough love,
but he was hurt, and he knew how to hurt his
family.

That is all history now,
he has changed and is very loving.
The differences cannot be contrasted in words.

The days have gone by,
the wounds are healing and recovering.
Now it is time to feel human.

It is my time to learn to live,
like someone who knew what a childhood was;
like a true human who was not denied life.

I knew words were powerful;
that violence was not the answer,
and my family is a living example of this.

A Blessing For My Mother

The role of a mother,
can be fulfilled by no other.
Taking care of the family,
to her, it is not a bit of a bother.

She is like a sapphire;
if my life is a bike, she, is its tyre.
Her smile is so very beautiful,
that it sets my heart on fire.

Her presence fills my sight,
it cures the confusion of the night.
What a rare gem is she,
being my shadow in the broad daylight.

Filled with compassion and love,
to you, my dear mother I bow.
May the Almighty bless you from the skies
above,
bring goodness to you on the wings of a dove.

The Tale Of The Fallen

Life, it isn't easy at all,
there was no one when I had a fall!

Tears fell from my eyes day and night,
my adrenaline was on fight or flight.

With a shattered heart, soul depressed,
all my emotions were uncontrollably
suppressed!

Unable to carry the broken me,
I fell into a ditch and couldn't see.

I wondered if life was worth,
my heart said yes although it was hurt!

Breaking the walls of the ditch,
I was all in cuts and bruises.

Lifting myself up gently,
I started being stable mentally.

Believing in myself, I took a step,
and it helped me climb up to success!

I constantly slipped down,
my face showing sadness and frown.

Listening to my heart, I moved forward,
I proved to myself that I am not a coward!

Yes, I was bruised and hurt,
but I wasn't in the ditch full of dirt!

That is when I noticed I am wow,
I was strong and unbreakable now!

Finally, I picked myself back up without harm,
standing strong even in the storm.

From the beginning, till the end,
God was my strength, my best friend.

He helped me pick myself up, when I was fallen,
and that is how it ended; The tale of the fallen.

The Eagle

I was alone.
They heard my screams; they saw me torn apart,
but all they did was listen
and laugh about my brokenness.

I learnt not to expect,
also, that no one cares.
I was hopeless and depressed.

I did not know I did not need them;
that I could gladly protect myself.
I knew that ghosts may be scary,
but humans were definitely scarier.

This was what I got,
but that was not what I would become.
I turned out to be different.

Like an eagle I flew high,
I regrew my beak,
I restored my talons.

Making sure I had a vision,
I stepped ahead overcoming my challenges.
I knew I could win.

I was alone.
They heard my success; they saw me at the top,
but all they did was listen,
and laugh making up rumours.

I learnt to give with no bounds,
also, to listen and empathise.
I made myself the softest, yet so durable.

I could be there for many,
and comforted the cries of the disheartened.
I know that people may be ruthless,
but definitely I was compassionate,
and in the end, discovered myself.

Wake Up

Girls and boys, it's time to wake up
into the world that is changing.

Be ready to face new situations,
otherwise, time will pass by.

Prepare yourself to see the change,
in the way the world sees you.

You are growing older;
remember to be responsible for yourself.

Being judged now will be difficult,
but do your best in front of others.

Your teenage is coming to an end;
push yourself because no one will.

Be healthy, maintain your body as you grow,
you will regret if you don't do it now.

Find joy in helping others,
because what you sow you reap.

Be the light to the world,

you are the youth of the present.

Don't let the process change you,
strive to be the best out there.

The Cloth That Was Washed

Getting out of pain
is like a stain on a cloth.
It is hard to take it off,
but easy to make.

Based on its diversity,
All it may need is some water
Or it may need some soap;
Similar to a heart with trauma in it.

It takes efforts to wash,
but eventually it will go away.
Not all stains go away,
some stay forever, but are not so visible.

The faster you notice it,
The better you wash it, the easier to erase.
Sometimes you figure it out later on,
and it takes time, but it will get better.

Make sure to scrub it gently,
but let your soap be the most effective.
Do not be too harsh,
Or the threads may wear out.

Because the threads are made
with utmost thought by its creator,
so that it can add beauty
to the entirety of this universe.

Never let that stain be yourself,
but let it be a part of you,
which is not just something to be removed,
but something that once withstood
embarrassment,
and got over pain,
like the cloth that was washed.

Gratitude

Sometimes it is all about being grateful.

For the little good morning by your neighbours,
and your dog that follows you around in the
morning.

For the driver that safely leaves you to college,
and your friend that warmly greets you with a
smile so adorning.

For the people in your surroundings that give
you their times,
and your food that gives you energy for the day.

For the buildings that protect you from the
weather
and your clothes that provide comfort.

For the trees that you pass by daily,
and your books that offer knowledge.

It is these small things that bring true joy,
and I hope you notice them.

May it bring a beautiful smile on your face,

with wholesome gratitude to it all.

You And Me

Your miraculous power, it saved me.
Your unending mercy, it loved me.
You told me that I am yours,
and my darling, you are mine.

No words can describe your true love.
The way you caress me, your gentle touch,
you are my beloved, my everything.
Only tears can express my love for you.

When I was born, you were dedicated to support
me.
You carved my name on your palm, so
beautifully.
You raised me up, when I was down,
you made me win, when I was lost.

I cried, and you heard my cries,
and when I did not, you heard my silence.
My redeemer, my best friend;
although I have never seen you, you were
always by my side.

Never let me go, always hug me tight;
Even if I try to escape from your purest love.

It is my greatest desire, my forever yearning,
to meet you and be one with you, my God.

39

www.ingramcontent.com/pod-product-compliance
Lightning Source LLC
LaVergne TN
LVHW051237200726
843510LV00011B/1592